T0146569

A Changed Heart

*An intimate look into a
pregnant 15 year old's
journey through life and loss.*

NATASHA GRANTZ

WESTBOW
PRESS®
A DIVISION OF THOMAS NELSON
& ZONDERVAN

Scripture taken from the King James Version of the Bible.

This book is a work of non-fiction. Unless otherwise noted, the author and the publisher make no explicit guarantees as to the accuracy of the information contained in this book and in some cases, names of people and places have been altered to protect their privacy.

Photography by Roxanne Allenbaugh
(for Author photo and 'Photo 10')

WestBow Press books may be ordered through booksellers or by contacting:

WestBow Press
A Division of Thomas Nelson & Zondervan
1663 Liberty Drive
Bloomington, IN 47403
www.westbowpress.com
1 (866) 928-1240

ISBN: 978-1-5127-4312-8 (sc)

Print information available on the last page.

WestBow Press rev. date: 7/6/2016

To my first-born son, Brandon.
You are just as special as we
imagined you would be.

Love you,
Mom

The following is a large portion of a letter I wrote to my son's late father, Brandon. He was shot and killed on August 13th, 2003 when I was five months pregnant with our son. It was eight days before my 16th birthday. Writing to him worked as a way for me to vent and move through the stages of grieving more easily. I began writing shortly after he passed and I concluded it several years later in 2007, right before I began college. In August of 2015, after the letter was long forgotten, I found it tucked away in my moms attic. I decided to turn it into a book in order to keep Brandon's memory alive for our son and to help those who may feel like life is over after facing a traumatic event. Although this letter is a reflection of my testimony in itself, I've also shared my full testimony in hopes that those who do not know Jesus, would be inspired to get to know Him.

This letter is by no means intended to encourage teen pregnancy. In fact, I believe we should prevent it to the best of our abilities by educating young girls about their true value. Knowing who they are in the eyes of God is critical to them respecting themselves as well as their bodies. That's where it all begins...

The names of the people included have been changed in order to protect their privacy.

Contents

Chapter 1 1

Chapter 2 14

Chapter 3 18

Chapter 4 23

Chapter 5 25

Chapter 6 28

Chapter 7 32

Chapter 8 33

Chapter 9 35

Chapter 10... 37

Chapter 11 40

Chapter 12 43

Chapter 13 45

Chapter 14... 47

Chapter 15 49

Chapter 1

Brandon,

I don't even know where to start. I never thought I would be writing a letter like this to you. This is so hard to believe and I'm still having a hard time dealing with it. It seems like yesterday when you would bust into my room in the morning and lay next to me. It seems like yesterday when we would argue over things that weren't worth it. It seems like yesterday we would just sit there and stare into each other's eyes. We were so close it made people sick.

I can't do anything without thinking about you. I can't look at newspapers, hear or see ambulances, or even listen to the radio because every song is our song.

When I think about the day it happened, I can barely breathe. I remember it like it happened one minute ago. My mom came in the house and told me she heard on the scanner that there were two males down between 15th and 4th. Usually I wouldn't think much of it, but when she told me, my heart dropped.

First I paged you to make sure you were ok, like I always did, but you didn't call back. I thought you were being stubborn because we were arguing. We went down to the 18th street ball field to try and find out what happened because that's where a Life Flight helicopter was landing. When it landed, I began to cry. I had no idea who was hurt at this point, but I just got this feeling that wherever *you* were, you weren't ok.

I remember thinking, *what's wrong with me? I don't even know what happened.* I guess I was thinking the worst: what if it was you?

We walked home and met Whitney walking down our street. I ran up to her and asked, "Who was it, who got shot?" She told me "B." I told her to stop playing around because I didn't believe her. When she started crying, I knew she was serious.

Me, Whitney and my mom got into the jeep and went down toward the scene. When I saw Marcus, I asked him who it was and he just said "B, your boy." I'll never forget that moment...I just put my head down. It was all too hard to believe. It seemed like the beginning of a bad dream.

We went home to find out more information: What hospital were you in? Were you even in one? I just kept praying and praying that if God gave you another chance, I would try even harder to pull you away from the street life. You were too good for that life anyway and always talked about making a real change now that I'm pregnant.

Anyhow, I heard it was either you or the other guy involved who died. It seemed like everyone was hiding something from me. Like they already knew it was you and they were scared to tell me.

I was still in shock at your funeral. I just kept thinking *ok I know he's lying in a casket, in this church with flowers all around him, but I know my baby isn't dead.* I tried to convince myself that you were just sleeping. I stared at your chest waiting for it to move up and down, but it never did and my pain grew worse. Then I just kept waiting for you to get up and for someone to explain why they had to fake your death. As time went on, reality hit me in waves. This wasn't a bad dream—I wasn't going to wake up and find you next to me.

I know you thought I lost the bracelet you gave me, but I didn't. I just said that because I was mad at you, but I put it back on and I'm never taking it off again. I'm also keeping everything else you've ever bought me. Every single thing. I want you to know that I love you, and I can never put into words just how much. I miss everything. I am so used to seeing you every day and acting stupid together— like farting and blaming it on each other all the time. Remember around the time around when we first met and I fell down the steps? You tried so hard not to laugh, but you sure did start crackin' up. Remember the night you threw up and I took care of you? You know I have to love you because you and everyone else knows how I feel about throw up! That was the same night my friend Kara came over and we stayed up all night talking about everything—things that bothered us in life, things that made us happy (like each other). We laughed so hard the whole night.

Remember we used to go to the movies every single Saturday? Eventually we always argued over who was going to get up and get the newspaper to see what was playing.

I loved our long, deep talks. I miss being on the phone with you all night. We used to be on the phone forever talking about everything and anything we could think of. We talked about how you never

3

wanted our baby to ever have to work a day in their life, but I always said they needed to be independent when they're older. I think they should work for what they want.

I know how much you loved me. Everyone always talked about how mean you were to other girls and how good you treated me. I will never forget when your cousins pulled up in the car and saw us playing in the snow outside. They always made fun of you for it. We have so many good memories. I'll never forget you trying to sing to me either. Even though you couldn't sing, it was so cute.

I know if you're watching me from Heaven, you were probably laughing at me at the funeral because I kept messing with Sierras's cousin's flowers. Kara and I took her letter out of your casket and read it. I was scared there might be something in there I didn't know about you guys, but it was just random stuff about you two being good friends.

What hurts the most is that I know if you were still alive, we would be super close. Remember when I told you about my dream that you got shot? It was one of those dreams that seem so real, like its actually happening. I called you in the morning to come over, and I couldn't stop hugging you. I was so happy the dream wasn't real. I kept making you promise you would be there when the baby was born, because I had a deep feeling that you wouldn't be. Not that you wouldn't want to be—you were more exited than I was, but I kept getting a feeling that you wouldn't be *able* to be there. I needed to hear you promise. So much was left unsaid...I hate this so much.

The last time we talked was two days before it happened—the longest we ever went without talking. I never got to tell you that I had to go to the hospital later the same day as our argument because I was having pains. The doctors gave me medicine because the baby was too low. My mom wanted me to call you, but I didn't want to because I was being stubborn. I should have. I would give anything now to just be able to hug you again. Part of me wishes I was there when it happened because I wanted to be one of the people telling you to breathe again, but seeing you take your last breath would have literally killed me too! I would have lost my mind. My heart is so shattered... I have never felt such intense pain in my life.

I always think about the first day we officially met. We went to see *Darkness Falls* at the movies. On the way there, you told me how pretty you thought I was. When you asked me for a kiss, I was so nervous. That's all I talked about when I got home, and my mom kept teasing me about it. I never started liking someone so much in one day. The next movie we saw was *How to Lose a Guy in 10 Days* and you kept asking if I was trying to lose you in ten days. Haha you always kept me laughing. I could see how happy it made you when I would smile.

When we first talked on the phone before we met, I didn't like the way you sounded. I could never understand what you were saying because of your Detroit accent. After a while, I had to translate what you were saying to other people. It was hilarious. What I wouldn't do to hear your voice just one more time...

I'm not used to being away from you for this long. I wish I could talk to you about how you feel and how it happened. What was going through your head? I wonder if your life really flashes before your eyes. I had a dream we were in my room and I asked you if you went to Heaven. I was asking you all about it, but you were sad and wanted to go back to where the light was. We weren't speaking out

5

loud using real words; it was like we were talking in our minds. It was the weirdest thing ever, but it still felt like being right there with you. Then I started crying really hard, and you said, "Come on now sweetheart don't cry." I wonder if that was really you, and I wonder if that's how people talk in a spiritual world—just in their heads and hearts.

Remember the funny songs I would make up for you? "Forget the A forget the C, I love my B." I can't wait to take care of our baby. It's going to be hard watching them take their first step without you there—or when they smile for the first time or say their first word. I'm going to tell our kid all about you when they're older. If a little kid in their school ever says something smart about it's dad being dead or hurts their feelings, that's just going to crush me. There's still a long way before he or she is here though.

I just took a break from writing and went to Golden Dawn with my mom. Everywhere I go, a billion things remind me of you. I have so much to deal with down here, but when my day comes, wait for me at the gates. It's going to feel so good to run into your arms and to see that huge bright smile of yours again!

I try to hold in my tears all the time, but I just can't. I have never heard or seen so many people crying at the same time like at your funeral. Hearing grown men cry so loud is a sound I will never forget. Ever. It's really scary. I wonder if it sounds like that in Hell—people just crying and screaming so loudly in pain. I'm reading this book called *We are Eternal*. The author said, "When someone touches our life briefly but profoundly, how much greater are the lessons?" He also said that when children die, their lives are "like a stone hitting a pond: they make a big splash in this world and no matter how short or long their physical life, theirs is like a ripple that touches many" (Brown, Robert. (2004). *We Are Eternal.* Grand Central Publishing. I like that because that's how your life was even though you were an adult. You made a splash in the world when you were born since your mom had issues with pregnancy and even births before. You changed her life and showed her how powerful the love is between a mother and child. You showed your cousins that love between you all is just like love between brothers, and you showed me that there are guys out there who would treat me well, unlike my ex-boyfriend. It's going to be hard taking care of our baby without you. I will have a lot of support, but they can't give him or her fatherly love like you would.

You and I used to have so much fun together. I just keep trying to think of all the funny times to help me get through this pain. I think about how you would always scream to random dudes walking by and tell them I wanted to talk to them. You thought it was hilarious since you only said it to the not so cute, ones.

Remember when you flipped out on my neighbor for walking around outside with his shirt off? All because he used to like me and you thought he was just trying to show off his muscles for me.

You know what else hurts me along with everything else? I feel like you are fading away in my mind as the months go by. Maybe it's meant to be that way, but it hurts. The other day my nephew asked if you were in the sky and when I told him yeah he said, "Him's in Heaven?" I used to always say I didn't have a life because you and I never went out, we just stayed in like an old couple. Now I realize I did have a life, and *now* it feels like I don't.

My mom and I were just talking the other day about when I first found out I was pregnant. You guys went for a ride to talk about it and you were telling her about how I was so mature for my age and different from every other girl you ever met. It was so funny when you forgot your ID at my house and she finally found out how old you were. Little did she know, I lied to you at first about my age too.

Remember you told me your plan was to "mold" me because I was younger, but it backfired because you fell in love? Your mom told me about when you called her too and told her you met "the one." Then she cussed you out when you told her my age.

I can't believe you're actually in a whole different dimension than I am. You couldn't possibly be any further away. I don't know what the outcome of all this will be, but I feel like I'm going to explode. I get so frustrated and cry over and over again. All I want is for you to show me something. Show me that you're ok and make it so real that I don't have to question whether it was a real experience or not. The fact that you're gone makes me so sick to my stomach. Physical pain is nothing compared to this feeling. Getting shot ten times in each of my arms and legs or being stabbed would still hurt less than this.

Your mom just got here from Detroit. It's so hard looking at her because you can see all the pain in her face. I can't even imagine how she feels...I wish I could do something for her.

Sometimes, I don't want to be bothered by anyone else except her. I especially can't stand people who say nice things or try to pretend they understand, because they don't. I know I'm young and no one takes what we had seriously, but when you're with someone every single day and all of a sudden they're gone, it hurts so much. No one but us needs to know just how close we really were anyway.

I went through a phase where I was mad at you for leaving us. I know that's weird and maybe even stupid, but I did. Your mom's boyfriend told me, "You have to remember, it isn't his fault he left." He didn't even know I was feeling that way. What's going to hurt the most is having to tell our baby that they will never meet you on this earth. You'll never be able to pick them up and hug them, and that kills me.

My mom gets mad at me when I don't accept people's phone calls. I wish she wasn't like that. This is my way of learning how to deal with what happened. I don't feel like people should get upset with me. The people who call can't bring you back and don't give me the help I need, so why talk to them? Now is not the time. I'm not even myself anymore, anyway. Whitney said she feels like she lost her best friend after what happened, and she really did. I need help or I'm going to go crazy. I honestly don't feel like I'm healthy enough to have a baby living off of me right now. Don't get me wrong, I love our baby already, but I just don't feel like my body is healthy enough to support him or her to grow. I don't know what to do; I'm super scared that this is all going to affect them. I'm scared of a lot of things actually. One of the things that make me feel better is looking at my stomach while the baby's moving. I hate that you can't see it, but at least you got to feel it before and you were so excited the first time. I'll always remember that look on your face.

Sometimes, I feel like this is all my fault. If we weren't arguing you probably would have been at my house that night. Why *that* night out of all nights? I don't understand why he shot you in the chest. I don't understand why it couldn't have just happened to be somewhere else. I know we made stupid mistakes, but we were too close for something like this to happen—for us to be torn apart forever.

I still don't know the full story about why it all happened in the first place. All I know is everyone said you, your cousins and Trevon, the guy that shot you – were sitting on Marcus' mom's porch. Supposedly, you all were just laughing and cutting up. Then you and Trevon got into an argument over something dumb so you guys went into the alley to fight. I guess things escalated from that point on. Someone told me there were kids looking out a window in one of the houses and you were screaming for them to get down when you realized Trevon pulled his gun out. I want to know the full exact story with every single detail though. I don't deserve to be left in the dark.

I don't know how, but I swear I knew you wouldn't be there when the baby was born. Even though you told me, "Sweetheart, stop. You know I'm going to be there," a million times, my feeling just wouldn't go away.

It was funny how you used to tell me to eat healthily and eat foods that you liked because you were convinced that the baby already liked all the same foods as you. I miss you always asking, "How are both of my babies doing?" I also miss when you used to get mad when I didn't give you that certain look you use to call "the love look."

I'll never forget when you bought me that bracelet and brought it over right after your court hearing. You were so happy you didn't get locked up, and you looked so cute and skinny in your little suit. You promised me you would be there right after court and you sure were. Every time you couldn't get the car to come see me you would call and we would stay on the phone all day and night.

I keep playing out fake scenarios in my head about what life would be like if you lived. I see myself in the hospital with you, never leaving your side. I was just looking at your death certificate, and my heart drops every time I read about the bullet piercing your lung. Why do I keep reading it? I think to myself *wow a little piece of metal took his whole life away.* When I saw the "Late Deaths" section in the newspaper and read your name, I just died inside. I see, "Brandon Lockett" and it just doesn't make sense. Not *my* Brandon.

I hate how I can't call you anymore to make all my problems better. All I have is this letter to share my thoughts. Even though I know you'll never get it, it helps so much to vent to you. When I woke up in the morning, you were always the first thing on my mind, and I was so happy when you told me the same thing. When I went shopping, I always thought about if you would like what I was buying. When I bought new make up, I couldn't wait to try it on to look good for you and when we weren't together, I was always anxious to get back to you. Maybe we both had a feeling deep down that our time together might be short since we always hugged and kissed a few extra times when we said goodbye.

You used to always ask if you were a good boyfriend. I never knew why you always asked, but you really were. You always cared about my feelings, never left me if I was upset about something, and you put up with so much!

One of my best memories of you is from when we were in that stupid purple van and we were riding back to New Ken from Vandergrift. I know we made that trip lots of times but this time, we were coming up over a hill and the sun shone on your face. I don't know why that moment sticks out in my mind so much, but it does. I guess it was just something about the way you looked. My heart went crazy inside. It hurts that we can't make new memories and I have to just dwell on the ones we already have.

I get weekly emails to tell me how the baby is doing and this one says, "Here's tips to help dad prepare." It hurts reading it. You were always so interested in everything about the baby. Remember you used to sleep with your hand on my stomach because you didn't want to miss a movement? I know you would have been the best father in the world. You had such a good heart, even if only a few people saw it.

Every day I have hope that the next day will be different. I want to wake up and see some of your stuff around and see ten missed calls from you on my phone as usual. I have no idea why I hold onto this. I need to accept it because every day it's the same. I just want to blink my eyes and be wearing the blue dress I had on the night you left. I want to see the same people who were at my house that night, and then be able to run to you just in time and change everything before it happened. I just want to rewind time. I see the movies we saw in theaters coming out on DVD now, and it is killing me that life went on. Life wasn't supposed to go on... how could it?

Anyway, I think we are going to have my baby shower at the end of November—make the lights go out or something crazy. I wish you could be there and be all annoying asking what everything is and what it does. It's true you never know what you got until it's gone. I remember you saying that to me before when you thought I was going to break up with you.

I can't stress just how much I miss you....
I knew you loved me even before the first time you told me. You always told me how sick you would be without me. I picture us all together and our kid is older and leaving the house as we tell them, "Be careful." I hate knowing that will never happen. I just sit here

and look at pictures of you wishing I could literally jump into it just for a second to go back to that day. I always felt so good about myself when I was with you too. I have to go, but will write again soon. I love you.

Chapter 2

I'll never forget the first time I saw you. I was in the car with my boyfriend at Sheetz. He was getting gas and I saw you walk into the gas station and thought to myself, *that's the finest dude I've ever seen.* The next week your cousin ran up to me in school saying you wanted to talk to me. Then I found out it was you—the same guy from Sheetz. I still don't know how you even knew me, but the rest was history. Before long, you and your boys were trying to beat my now, ex boyfriend up and chasing his car on your bikes. That was hilarious. Anyhow, your mom gave me your coat, which was the same one you were wearing that day at the gas station. I'm keeping it forever.

I hate that I'll never be able to cook for you again and how we can't play *Michael Jackson Moonwalk* on Sega all night anymore. I used to think I was so grown and so mature for my age, but I have yet to experience real life until now. It's not just about preparing for motherhood... it's the experience of losing someone so close that is forcing me to wake up.

It breaks my heart when I think about our kid starting school. I think about things like what if they have Bring Your Dad to School Day? There's so much I think about, and they aren't even born yet.

I loved how respectful you always were to my parents. Even the one time when my dad was trippin' cause you tried to come over all late. I always snuck you in anyway, but still. I want the life we always said we were going to have: getting married, having a ton of kids and living in a house that had a white picket fence.

Ever since this all happened, my perspective on life has totally changed. I used to have so many questions, and it seemed like everything was so confusing. Now I think it's definitely love that keeps the world going around. The answer is simple.

I know this may sound weird, but I really never thought much about death, or maybe I didn't care. I don't know. When I would hear something on the news like someone got shot or a plane full of passengers crashed I would say, "Aww, that's sad." I never wondered how their friends and families must have felt. When Sept 11th happened, I didn't even try to imagine how they must have felt. But now, I do know and I can imagine at least a little of their pain. It hurts beyond belief...an unbelievable insane amount of pain. I just want to talk to you. The night it happened, I sat in the bathroom and just cried and begged God to let you be alive. Now I hate going into the bathroom; I feel that deep sorrow in my heart all over again. Every room has a bad memory of that night and it's still so clear in my mind.

Everything got so much worse too when my friend Nicole came over. I knew she would be the one who knew exactly what was going on. I just kept literally running away from her because she was crying and I didn't want to hear what was going to come out of her mouth. I knew hearing her say it would make it real. I wanted her to tell me that you were in the hospital and ask me if I needed a ride there, but she didn't. Finally she just said it, and I swear I got dizzy and the room spun like in the movies. I should have paged you our secret code for I love you: "143." First we were all running around trying to figure out what happened and the phone was ringing off the hook. Then she just came over and confirmed everything. I wasn't ready for that.

I hate knowing you died in a painful way. We were supposed to go to Idlewild the day of your funeral. It would have been our first time going to an amusement park together. You weren't supposed to die. I hate how life is so unpredictable. Everywhere I go, I feel hurt; every time I open my mouth to speak (whether its about you or not), I have to calm myself down first because I get a lump in my throat. I want to be little again with no cares in the world—back to the Barbie days when everyone was a best friend, boys had cooties, and we wondered what tampons were.

When I get to Heaven, I want to talk for hours and then you can introduce me to 2pac—if he really is dead. I miss your gorgeous face. I miss looking into your eyes...they were so beautiful, I always loved how they were shaped. I loved your dark shiny hair, long eye lashes and I even loved the birthmark on your back that reminded me of the Penguin's logo. I never want to forget any details about you.

You know how I take breaks from this letter and write whenever? Well I was just sitting here playing a game on the computer a few minutes ago, and I just heard on the news that Trevon was charged for your death. Every time I hear about you being gone, it feels like the first time. People cried at your funeral, then went home and went about their days, but your mom, your cousins and I can't have it like that. It never ends.

I'm going to name the baby LaShaye if it's a girl. I really don't like it, but your mom was going to name you LaShaye if *you* were a girl. She would love it if I used that name. My mom likes it a lot too, but I think it's a boy! I hope so. I want to teach him how to treat girls. I would adore having a son.

Your mom is such a strong and beautiful woman, by the way. If it weren't for her, I would be way worse than what I am right now. Instead of this getting easier every day, I feel like it's getting harder. I haven't written as often as I usually do lately and I'm feeling more and more down. Having this baby is going to make me feel so much better but I'm still going to feel like I'm drowning in sadness.

I love how you used to always say you're glad you're having a baby with me, even though it was unplanned. You were so happy about it. I never planned on having kids at all, especially not this young. It helps that we were so close before I got pregnant though. Sometimes I just want to trash everything that you bought me, and everything that reminds me of you, and just burn it—but I can't.

I'm sick of everyone telling me to do this and that so the baby is healthy. What makes people think you can really control yourself in a situation like this anyway?

Chapter 3

It's October 29th and I just found out it's a boy! After she told me it was a boy she said, "Oh and look at that big toe!" I didn't tell her he got that big toe from me. Renee always said my big toes were huge and looked like chicken nuggets. She's funny... my toes aren't *that* bad. You always said my feet were pretty. Anyhow, your family is so happy. Since you said it has to be a junior if it's a boy, it looks like he will be Brandon DeShaye Lockett Jr.

I'm so anxious to have him so I can hold him. I just talked to your mom; she's having another bad day. I hate hearing her so sad... You meant so much to her; you can tell she loved you more than life. She told me today, "I'm so happy Brandon picked you. He chose a wonderful young lady and I just love you." It made me feel good, but I'm still so emotionally messed up. I always think *what if something happens to my brain* since I feel like it's on overload.

I still read a lot of books about spiritual stuff. I've been reading a lot about angels lately. Some say they aren't boys or girls and some say they can be either. I don't know what to believe. I just like reading this stuff and talking with mediums online to see if anyone can give me a message from you. I need to feel like you're close.

The baby shower was yesterday. I got almost $600 plus over $200 in gift cards and a ton of gifts. Your mom made me carry around all my cards and stuff in a big bag so no one could steal it. I felt so dumb lugging it around. I have a lot to do to prepare for him, but I guess it will keep me busy.

I'm going to be such a good mom even though I'm young. I'm already proud of myself. The baby's nursery looks so nice! I did a "blue jean teddy" theme. Everyone loves it.

I had another dream about you last night. It was different than all the other ones, and it felt so real. You were standing by the window and everything was just so beautiful. I felt like I was in Heaven too. The atmosphere was different and I was asking you about being there again. You seemed so happy and peaceful, and I woke up with such a good feeling in my heart. It was the first time I had peace since you left.

Christmas is coming up, and I'm going to JcPenney to finish shopping. Maybe I'll find another gift for your mom because I already got her some nice perfume. I don't know if it's going to be her Christmas or birthday present yet since they're so close.

Well it's about time where I can honestly say I'm officially grown— kind of. This is the first year where I don't care about Christmas. Well I do care, but I'm not looking forward to it I guess. I don't know if it's because I'm having a baby or what. I think its because I'm not happy. How can I even enjoy the holiday? At least the baby brings me happiness and helps fill the giant hole in my heart, even though he's not here yet. I feel like it's just hard to care about stuff anymore. I always feel like crying. It's so hard without you. Who is Bonnie without Clyde or Corey without Topanga? Ok we're not exactly like any of them, but you know what I mean.

Man these books I'm reading talk a lot about reincarnation, but if you ask me, I don't think it even makes sense. Supposedly, no matter how many times you reincarnate, you are still the same person. Wouldn't that mean our individuality on this earth is taken away? They say "you are still the real you," but who is the real you then? I just came to the conclusion that no one knows anything for sure. Just because mediums say they talk to people from the other side doesn't mean they actually know what's on the other side. Those are two completely different things. Maybe they don't even talk to dead people at all, who knows?

I still think about you every second. My body gets exhausted, but my mind just won't shut off. I know it was your time. It had to have been. Anyhow, I just sent your mom some of the poems I wrote. I hope she likes them. I shared them with a few people before, and no one believed that I actually wrote them. I guess that means they're good huh?

When our son is born, I don't want everybody all up in his face. I just want it to be him and me. I don't want anyone near him, and I won't trust anyone with him unless we are really close.

I keep reading these books written by some psychic lady too. I want to believe some of the stuff, but other things are just so weird. I don't want to picture you as some transparent spirit or a little ball of light flying around. I'd give anything to turn around and have you here again. I cried my eyes out again last night and still have the worst headache. On a brighter note, your mom got my poems and said she loved them. She thinks they're beautiful and I should try to write for Hallmark. I'm glad she liked them so much. I didn't want them to make her more upset.

Well I always used to say that whenever I have kids, I want to look the best pregnant, but I guess that went down the drain, huh? At least this will be a one-time thing because I'm not having any more kids.

I want this baby to come so I can stay up all night taking care of him instead of staying up all night wondering what things are going to be like during labor. I'm scared. I still didn't get sick though. I never got sick at all, thank God!

Last night I was just lying there thinking *ahhh I can't wait until he comes back.* It's like one minute I face reality, and the next minute I'm in a fantasy tricking my brain into believing you're here still somehow. I get extremely frustrated with people when they don't understand my pain, but I know it's not their fault. I still haven't had a full night's sleep since you left. Its like my body realizes something in life is wrong, and I just automatically wake up all the time. I know I'll never find anyone like you again.

I've been thinking about Hell a lot lately too for some reason. I don't think people who commit suicide always go to there. No one knows for sure... would if they just had a serious mental illness? God knows more about their minds and hearts than we do. There's so much we don't have the answers to. One thing's for sure, I hope people don't just sit around playing harps all day in Heaven. That would be so boring. I wrote this poem since I've been thinking about spiritual stuff lately...

> *What we know is what we see*
> *When your eyes don't provide it for you,*
> *What decision will it be?*
> *Do you feel the need to question*

21

Or is your instinct to believe?
When you cannot look upon God's face
Do you say He's nonexistent
Or dedicate your heart to faith?
Is there a Heaven, although you can't see its gates?
Do you question the life and death of our complex human race?
When you cannot find the answers on pages in books
Will you come to believe or continue to look?
When you continue to search and find not a thing
Will you still then deny our Lord and King?

On a different note, everyone keeps saying the baby is going to have a lot of hair when he's born because I always get heartburn so bad. Well for all this, he better have enough to get it braided when he comes out.

Chapter 4

It's 8 in the morning now and I still haven't gone to sleep. I think my TV broke so I came downstairs at 2:30am because I can't sleep without it on anymore. I can't deal with the silence and being stuck alone with my own thoughts.

Remember when I snuck you in the one time and me and Kara had to leave you here when we went to Sheetz? I was scared to get caught because you would always be snoring so loud or laughing at the TV like you were at your own house. We hated being away from each other though so the risk was worth it.

I feel like no one is supportive when I really need it. Obviously I made bad decisions in life, but everyone else my age does too. Its like people don't want their daughters around me, but their daughters are doing the same exact things! Some do even worse! The only difference is that I got caught. Everyone just distances themselves and talks about me. They treat me like I'm some evil witch living in a village of perfect people. My biological dad doesn't even let my own sister talk to me. I'm supposed to be family; isn't it bad enough that he's already done so much wrong? He even told her and my brothers that I'll never finish high school or go to college and I'm going to be nothing in life. He talks about how my parents raised me "wrong," but how can he even say anything because he hid me from his family and didn't raise me at all? I just wish everyone would stop pushing me away! You definitely find out who is there for you and who isn't when stuff like this happens. A lot of my other family members stopped talking to me too, not just my biological family. My grandma, my dad's step-mom, has been really supportive the whole time though. I really appreciate her. She's even making ceramics for me to give to your mom. One of them is a casino cup! You know how she loves going to the casino. I wish I were lucky. I can't even win at bingo.

Chapter 5

So now its 7:50 in the morning, and I didn't sleep last night either. I have a doctor's appointment today. Hopefully he says some type of action is happening. If he says nothing then I'll believe he's wrong because I keep feeling a lot of pain off and on. I don't think I'm really that big for being nine months pregnant, but I can barely shave my legs. I hate to say this, but sometimes I wish we never even met because this is way too painful. I just can't take this.

I hope our baby is born on Christmas, but then again I don't know about that. I'm thinking since a winter birthday would suck maybe we'll celebrate his birthday on your birthday, July 30th, every year instead. We'll see.

Anyway, it's funny how I get all these sympathy cards and flowers now, meanwhile half these people were fake chicken heads before you died. Now people just want to be in my face and pretend we were all close before. On a different note, I am sick of having to pee so much!

It's Christmas Eve and my mom keeps showing everyone the baby's room and how nice I made it look. Merry early Christmas, by the way. I wonder what Christmas is like in Heaven. Is it glorious? Do people even celebrate it at all there?

My uncle who had stopped talking to me finally talked to me again today. He asked me if I was ready to do all this, and then he made a smart comment. I know people want me to be so ashamed for having a baby young. Maybe I should be, but I'm really not. It happened and my mom and me just think we're going to make the best of this. What else can you do? I know I'll take good care of my baby. You know I have never been into drinking or partying anyway. I'm young, but I'm still not your average teenager. I don't have all the same interests as a lot of other girls my age. Plus, I know moms way older than me who are terrible mothers.

It's Christmas morning now. I remember the days when my mom used to wrap my stuff. It feels weird now knowing I'm having a baby. He's so low in my stomach, he feels like he's about to fall right out. I just talked to your mom. We have both been having such a rough time lately. This is all so strange and still so hard to deal with. Anyhow, I can't wait until the baby has his own little personality when he's older. I want to be able to say things like "he only likes his food cut this way" and "that is his favorite shirt." I just keep praying he will be 100% healthy! Remember when we were talking about how happy we were just over him having two arms and two legs? It seems like yesterday when I used to be so happy and free. I cared about simple, stupid things because there was nothing big to care about. Now I'm a single mom in pain starting a completely new life and not caring about who is calling or knocking on the door anymore. It's not so exiting now...

I just got back from the store. I got a $20 picture frame and blew our picture up to hang in the baby's room. We look so mean, but oh well. Hey why did I used to call you Mr. Boombostic? That's why you loved me I guess, since I was always crazy. I can't remember why I called you that though. Anyway, I will write again later. I love you, peanut head. Wait, speaking of peanut head, I forgot to tell you the baby looks like he has your head in the sonogram pictures! I think I'm going to have him today or tomorrow. I know I always think that; maybe I just have to poop. My due date, December 31st, is just two days away now!

Chapter 6

Well, I just went to my appointment; it's December 30th. The doctor said I need to go to the hospital now because I'm 2cm dilated. I'm so scared; I wish you were here for me to cry on! The next time I write, your son will be here. I love you. I miss you. I'm scared. I love you!

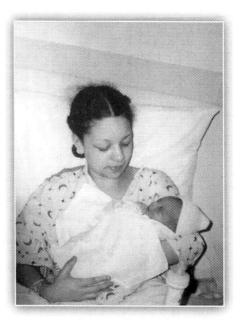

12/30/03 7lbs 14 oz.

He's here now! I'm not even going to describe the pain! They gave me medicine to move everything along more quickly. The nurses kept telling me I was still only 2 cm, but when they checked me they found out I was really 10cm so they rushed me to the delivery room. No one believed me that he was coming, and the doctor had the nerve to say I wasn't going to have him until the next day, but don't you know, he came at 10:23p.m that night. You both have birthdays on the 30th! I thought about you non-stop. I know you would have never left my side—not even for a second. He has your lips, forehead, skinniness, and nose of course. He's perfect! I still can't believe it. He has my chubby cheeks though, and that little dent above my top lip. It was horrible pain in that delivery room, but it was the best experience a person could ever have. I had so much support from your mom and my mom. You should have seen your mom's face in the delivery room though—she was mortified.

I wrote this poem about him...

> *Daddy's soulful eyes, full lips and pudgy nose*
> *Mommy's chubby cheeks and mommy's chubby toes*
> *Daddy's fingers, eyelashes and length*
> *Mommy's sweetness and daddy's strength*
> *Grandma's dimples and grandmas heart*
> *You are oh so precious, baby...*
> *You always were from the start*

"Mee maw" holding Brandon for the first time

I remember being happy just from seeing his arms and legs on the sonogram, so imagine how happy I am now to see all his fingers and toes in person. I have so many emotions right now! I hope your mom's heart gets a little lighter because I see all the pain she is still in. We always talk about how thankful we are that a baby came out of all this and we can have a piece of you. I love and miss you more than you will ever know.

Every time the baby squints his eyebrows, I think of you. Looking into his eyes feels so good. I never thought I would feel joy like this again. I'm still in a lot of pain though.

It's morning now and I feel like curling into a ball and dying. My body is so sore. I can't wait until the baby's crawling and laughing and doing all types of new stuff. He smiles in his sleep already so much. I didn't know babies did that.

I'm so sick of being in this house. At least before I had him, we were always out shopping and getting stuff ready, but now I have everything so we are just sitting here. I feel cooped up. I can't wait to be back to normal so I can move around better.

Your Aunt just called and was telling me all types of stuff your grandma said to do when babies cry. I feel guilty for not knowing all the tricks, even though I'm not expected to. My gram had eight kids, I think, and yours had ten. I wish I knew everything. I have so much to learn and I'm scared of the fact that I have to learn from experience. I don't want to get anything wrong with our baby.

Today is the 5th and I'm learning how to control my pain a little better. That's a really good thing, right? I love seeing the baby change every day. It's such a beautiful thing watching someone grow. I love and miss you more than anything. I think about you constantly.

Chapter 7

Happy Valentine's Day. I wish this day could pass just like any other day. Some of your family asked me to go out to eat, but I don't feel like it. I don't want to be around happy couples. I don't even want to see people kiss on TV anymore.

I deleted BET and MTV off my channel list because I don't want to take the chance of passing them and hearing one of our songs.

Chapter 8

Today is the 18th; it might just be the way winter skies are, but there's this one bright star and the whole sky looks so pretty. It makes me think of you...

Anyhow, I went to see *Passion of The Christ*. There were so many things running through my head about Jesus dying in such a horrific way. I know I'm not perfect and I'm not all religious and stuff, but that's messed up, man. I imagine how Mary must have felt watching her son die like that. I was bawling and people were coming out of the theater trippin and crying. I felt something, but I don't know what it was. It was deep though.

Good morning –

I really believe you literally just jumped on my bed. I just woke up and was lying under the covers and felt someone jump on the bed. I was about to flip out, but when I looked up no one was there. That was the craziest thing I ever felt. I physically felt someone jump onto the bed. My bed actually *moved* from the jump and I know I was fully awake so it's not like it could have been a dream. At first I was super scared and my heart just started beating all crazy, but then I calmed down and realized that had to be you. It was so sudden. Wow. I heard people talk about weird stuff like this before but I didn't believe them much until now.

I just saw a Big Red gum commercial, and of course that reminds me of you too since it was your favorite gum. I love our baby so much and he is so smart. It really hurts typing about him to you. It shouldn't have to be this way.

It's the 21st. The baby and I got our pictures done today, professionally. It felt so incomplete, but I still loved it. My sadness is turning into anger. When I see couples I act happy, but inside I think so many evil thoughts. Anyway, I have to go do homework and the baby is crying. I will love you with all my heart forever! I still don't know how I'm going to get through all this.

Chapter 9

I went to the park today to sit on our bench. Worms were out and you weren't there to give me a piggyback ride to the sidewalk. One had the nerve to be squirming by my foot. I got up and ran home like a killer was chasing me. Ughhh I hate worms and how they just pop up out of the ground and slither like that.

I feel like I'm on the road of life and my car is broken down. Some days are so much worse than others though. Every day has been bad this past week. Sometimes I feel like I don't even have the energy to do the simplest things. There better be a glorious world after this one to make up for all these hard times.

My nephew said he had a dream you came down from the sky in a box that had two holes in it. He's always walking around talking about you, and it's been so long since the last time he saw you. It was so funny when we used to babysit him and he would trash the whole house. He was a little terrorizer.

I used to feel so good when the sun would shine, and now I hate when it shines. It's like it's shining on some big happy world or something, and things are *not* happy here. I feel like it doesn't have the right to shine anymore. I always close the windows and doors. I miss sitting on the porch with you all the time. The weather was like this the day you left. I threw the dress I was wearing that day away. I never want to see it again.

Sometimes I feel like a failure, and I'm only 16. I just wonder if I have what it takes and have enough time to do everything I want to do in life. Everyone's always telling me what a great mom I am, and that I'm so beautiful, and this and that, but I feel so horrible inside. I love you, and I will love you forever.

Chapter 10

Today is April 22nd. I was thinking a lot in bed last night, like I always do, and I kept thinking about everything I've learned so far. I just want to improve myself from now on and keep these things in mind:

- Experience is the root of being wise.
- No matter how much you learn, you will never know everything.
- What goes around really does come back around, but it hits 100 times harder.
- Love is a very scary thing.
- No matter how straight your stuff is, it can all change in a matter of minutes.
- Don't trust people all willy-nilly.

I didn't make these up, but I like them a lot too:

- Anger is only one letter short of danger.
- If someone betrays you once it is his fault; if he betrays you twice it is your fault.

- Many people will walk in and out of your life, but only true friends will leave footprints on your heart.
- To handle yourself, use your head. To handle others, use your heart.
- Learn from the mistakes of others. You can't live long enough to make them all yourself.

Here are some of the poems I wrote too...

It won't happen to you
You're positive, you're sure
It's always the unimportant people
It's always the girl next door
It won't happen to you
You know it for a fact
But would if it did?
How would you react?
When you see others suffer
From a tragic loss
Do you honestly appreciate
All it is that you've got?

And since I love walking alone at night and looking at the stars, I wrote this one...

A sigh is what I give when I walk alone at night
When I try to tell myself everything will be alright
A sigh is what I give when I lay down in bed
And try to fight reality as memories dance through my head
A sigh is what I give when I look as far as I can see
It reminds me of the distance between you and me
A sigh is what I give when I look at the date and time

Our last moments together, still fresh in my mind
A very depressed sigh, is all that I can give
Because without you in my life, I don't think I can live

Today is April 26th. I keep having the same dream that all these different people are trying to shoot me. I hope the fear and pain you felt was nothing like it was in my dream. I need to see your face again. Anyway guess what? I got my permit today. I wore your socks for good luck. Creepy, I know. Anyhow, aren't you proud?

Today is May 2nd and why did Sierras's little cousin flip me off when she was driving away from the store? I'm 16 and she's like 20 something with a kid and she's really like that? She didn't even pay me her respects at the funeral. She's got some nerve. I know you guys had a past before but it wasn't even serious. We wont get into everything you told me about her though.

My mind has been so blank lately. I feel like such a robot. I hate how all types of serious things can happen when you least expect it. I would live in a shack with nothing if it meant I could just be with you again. Why can't I just have you back? Why did all this happen? It's so hard trying to be positive.

Yesterday was Mother's Day and I had an absolutely wonderful first Mother's Day. So many people told me, "Happy Mother's Day" and it just felt great. Your mom told me, "Now you put on something cute and take that baby for a walk." I love being a mom so much. Babies are so innocent and cute, how could people ever hurt children? They love and trust everyone. Adults should be like that. I love and miss you.

Chapter 11

Today is . . . I don't even know what day. I hate it that you're not here. A lot of people love the baby and me, but I still feel alone--like no one really cares that much.

I know I haven't written as much lately. I have so much homework, but I love schoolwork. I like challenging my brain and being distracted. I'm probably the only person ever who gets exited over new homework assignments. Anyway, I hope you always stay fresh in my mind as time goes on.

Brandon 7 months old

It's Tuesday, two days after Fathers Day. It wasn't as bad as I thought it would be. On a different note, sometimes I really don't want to raise our son here, Brandon. Someone's getting shot every other day now. It's always something. Clay was just shot and killed too. I want to call Jennifer and give her my condolences, but I know she probably doesn't want to hear it. I sure didn't. I didn't want people all up in my face. All I wanted was you. I feel so messed up right now. I can't even describe it. People are just dropping like flies left and right. I love you beyond words and I'll write later.

Today is July 29th, the day before your birthday. I just got back from your mom's house. Being in "The D" was so hard. I mean I knew it wasn't going to be great, but it was worse than I thought it would be. It broke me down! I was hoping your mom didn't see me crying, because I really didn't want to get into any conversations and start talking about stuff again. Then I would look at the baby's face and he'd be smiling, so I would smile and it just made me feel better.

I know if you were here you would have been showing me off all over the place and buying me anything and everything. You always said you were going to take me to Detroit and you wanted to take me shopping for something fancy so we could go to a play. I could picture you saying, "Aww, Sweetheart, you're in the D! Ain't she gansta'!" or some silly stuff like that. Everything about being there was tearing me up inside.

Ok so let's talk about this box of yours: the one I went through in your old room that you kept all your important stuff in. I can't believe you saved the card I got for you for your birthday. I read the long, mushy message I left in it. I got really overwhelmed when I read all of that. I started crying again when I found a picture of me. I saw your paper with all the Bible scriptures too. That is so cute that you used to write down your favorite verses and keep it like that. I got your compass too. Thanks, I always wanted one. I robbed your butt and you ain't even here. It's crazy that I have so much of your stuff, and even your son, but not you. I love you, Brandon.

Chapter 12

I just saw the picture that was taken on Charles' birthday. I can see you and your grandparents so well it's creepy! It's like the outline of your spirits but you can still see details! I swear I stopped breathing and I got a big lump in my throat. I just wanted to take that picture with me and go to our spot at the park and cry. I hate crying even more lately. I think a lot about how much you hated seeing me cry. Sometimes I just can't help it though. I wonder what's up with Heaven. How can people be all happy and jolly when they see people they loved down here hurting? Or maybe they don't see us at all. I don't know. Life is a you-know-what sometimes, man! My throat still has a lump in it. It's still hard for me to look at your pictures.

I want to go through this letter and read everything I wrote so far, but I'm scared because it's just going to crush my heart even more. Maybe I'll read it in a few years. I just want to type forever to keep you alive and fresh in my head. It's just too much! Anyway, happy birthday. I hated being at that little party your family had for your birthday. I felt so out of place and overwhelmed. I have to go. I'll write later. You've got my whole heart always and forever.

It's the 31st. I can't stop staring at this picture. It would turn people who don't believe in a spiritual world into believers. It's not one of those pictures where you can say, "Oh, well that's probably just smoke in the air or a glare from a TV, or the sun." It's a picture where you know what it is so you can't even lie to yourself. There's no point in even trying. I can't say I miss you enough. I feel like I'm living my life in a rush. Even though I don't want to die yet, you don't know how badly I want to see you again...how much I look forward to it.

8/4/04

I love our son so much, but being a single mom is starting to become depressing. I hate how you're not here. It's not like you're here and just a deadbeat dad. It's just not fair. I walk around every single day hurting. My body hurts physically too. This baby is heavy and my arms and shoulders are always hurting. I'm always tired and weak.

Chapter 13

11/2/05

Sorry I haven't written in a while. So much has been going on. My life has been crazy! I'm a senior now and I hate everybody in school. People are so immature and cold hearted, but I guess that's just high school for you. So anyway, I want to talk about this whole Roger thing. Your mom is happy for us, as I'm sure you already know. Your family is starting to understand. People in school judge everything because they don't have a life or anything better to do, of course. They don't know what it's like being in my shoes, but who are they to judge anyway...honestly. That is why all the nerds grow up and end up being rich and successful while everyone who made fun of them ends up still being lame. The nerds always mind their own business. Anyway, even though I shouldn't expect these young kids to understand the situation, I just hate seeing their faces every day. I can't wait to graduate. If your mom doesn't care then no one else should have a problem with it. We're really close and we don't understand *how*, just like no one else understands how. It is what it is though. He is familiar and reminds me of you. Most important of all, and like your mom said, I know I can trust him with the baby.

The few friends that I have crack me up. They are always talking about how he has such a gangster reputation, but his heart is so soft when it comes to me. He does so much good for the baby, and me and I know without a shadow of a doubt that he loves us above and beyond. It feels good to laugh so much again too. It's good for both of us. We still have bad days though. A few weeks ago, we just sat there crying for hours and talking about you.

I know how you would feel about us dating, and that's what gives me the most peace. You'd be happy as ever because you know how he loves our son. I'm a nice person just trying to live my life, not doing anything wrong, yet people can never shut up. They act like I'm a celebrity the way they are always up in my business.

I'm so glad I have good people in my life right now, especially Whitney. She's my best friend and knows me so well; it just feels good hearing her say she doesn't believe that I'm wrong. It gives me so much more confidence. She wants me to be happy. I love life and appreciate everyone and everything I have in mine right now, but the world is so messed up and hateful sometimes. It drains me. I know this probably sounds super corny, but I just want everyone to get along and stop hating on each other. I know the world will never be like that though. Anyway, I don't want to keep talking about all that stuff. I love you and I will write later!

Chapter 14

Well, I decided I'm going to go to the Art Institute. I am so happy about that. It's full of nice, but weird people--just like me! I will be in my "natural habitat" with other creative artists. I love interior design! I also feel guilty like maybe I'm meant to be doing something to help people in a bigger way instead. I just don't know exactly what that is. It's a really weird feeling. I have an urge to help as many people as I can in my lifetime, but I really don't know what to do.

I'm so proud of myself for making positive outcomes in all of this; I'm happy I made sure I learned from all that I went through. I feel like I learn something new in school and something new about life every day and I love it. I've always loved learning. Your mom has taught me so much too.

The baby is growing so quickly and he's so smart, as we all know. I'm not just saying that because he is my son either. He knows how to count to 15, he sings entire songs, answers the phone, and has whole clear conversations! It's like he skipped the baby talk. I'm not going to lie, it feels good having Roger around because I'm scared to experience all these things by myself. I don't want to, and I know he is just as interested in what he does as I am. Anyway, every time the baby does something cute or shocking, I wonder if you see it somehow. I really feel good getting all of this out.

Chapter 15

My lovely Brandon, it's been—what? A year since I wrote? So much has changed, including myself. I'm really finding myself and I have a new outlook on life. I'm so different from who I used to be when I first started this letter. Our son is so smart and amazing; I just have to say that again. It still hurts talking about him, but I have to tell you, he does so many new things every day. I love that boy so much!

The family is getting better about Roger and me. Well, they're getting better with me I should say. Some people still don't understand, but I'm not going to look down on them for it anymore. This is good for me because it shows me who's real and who isn't. I learned that it isn't right to judge people, and everything I've learned comes from living through so many things for myself. I have less than ten days til' I graduate high school, and we are having my graduation party on your birthday. It will be so nice to have everyone together that day.

Anyway, how about this one: Roger and I were walking and saw these easels that I wanted for my party to put all my pictures on, so we took them and ran home. My mom asked where we got them and when we told her, she told us it was a church. So we accidentally stole from a church. Nice. One way ticket to Hell, huh? We're going put them back. We are so crazy together, but I love how we are. It reminds me of us—the type of closeness we had. He smells like you too, and his arms and big hoodies remind me of you. I'm sure that's creepy, but at least it's comforting for me. I need this comfort.

7/30/06

I still think about you every single day. I'd rather have a thousand scars all over my body than this permanent scar on my heart. I'd go through anything over losing you. Anyway, it's your birthday. Of course I didn't forget. I thought today would be the perfect day to write. And since I haven't written after my graduation here it is...I officially finished high school! Roger cried at my graduation because he was so proud of me. I was really surprised, but it was nice to see how much he cares. Anyway, the baby is the cutest little boy ever and he talks so much. My eyes are tearing up now. He is perfect. I don't want to start crying a lot so I'll write again soon. I love you so much ... always and forever.

Roger and I just got back from vacation. I really missed my mom and the baby, but we are still depressed to be back in New Ken. We had a lot of fun going different places though. We went on boat rides and to a comedy show with a guy from BET there. Every night, we watched *Roseanne*. I think we saw every single episode. We caught a lizard in my aunt's pool, too. You should have seen how scared he was on the plane. It was his first time flying, and he wouldn't move his head off my lap. He wouldn't even talk...I swear he was about to cry. Anyway, it sucks being back here, but it was nice to get away. I think we both needed fresh scenery.

October 6th is my start date for college. I still have that really weird feeling that I'm supposed to be doing something much bigger, but it just doesn't make sense. I really do love design. I'm so ecstatic to be around other artists. It's us creative folk who have the biggest hearts. Anyhow, I know money isn't everything, but I wish I could give the world to everyone who was and is here for me through all of this—the people who loved me and never stopped supporting me regardless. They have no idea how much it means to me.

I was on the phone with Renee last night forever. We talked from 8pm to 6am about everything you could ever think of. We talked about us being biracial and issues we have, funny memories, our relationships and we even talked about God. It was such a deep talk, and I love that she and I can talk about anything. It feels good to be on a path to finding myself again. I still love and miss you more than words could ever describe, but I actually don't feel like a zombie anymore. I have a 4.0 GPA and I know what I want in life—I have goals. Having a kid motivated me so much too, it's crazy. I have never done this well in school before. I never cared to until now. I was never too ambitious, either. This feels really good! Anyhow, I'm so tired right now, but I'll write again soon. I love you, Brandon. You have so much to do with the woman I'm growing into.

PRESENT DAY

That was the last time I wrote in the letter. I didn't end it intentionally; it just came to a point where it felt as if life was moving forward. It wasn't always easy, but I did learn to accept it. I was also busy as I was preparing to start college. After I officially began, I had a new sense of clarity that I couldn't ignore. I was motivated, I was inspired, and I was confident. Life was good, and I only wanted it to get better from that point on. One of the changes I eventually felt I needed to make in order to stay focused was to break up with Roger. It was just too evident that we were on different paths in life, despite our bond at the time. I just couldn't see where he fit in the big picture I had painted for my future even after a few years of dating.

The most important change in my life, however, came two years later. It was the first day of the new quarter in school. I had just finished my afternoon class and was heading to my evening class not knowing what to expect. The name of the class was "Theory and Development of Form." I found the right room and quickly made my way to an empty stool. As I put my stuff down, I thought about how cool the room was in comparison to all my other classrooms. It was so industrial.

After I got situated, I looked up and saw our professor standing at his podium. He was focused on some paperwork and, once everyone arrived, he looked up and introduced himself. Instantly, I noticed there was something different about him. I was so taken aback by my weird, unexplainable observation; I mentioned it to the woman sitting next to me, a total stranger. For lack of better words, it seemed as if he was glowing. Not literally of course, but there was such a strong aura about him. It was so incredibly strange; it would have been too hard for me *not* to mention it to someone.

The woman next to me (who later became a very dear friend) responded to my comment without hesitation: "He's a Christian, that's what you see," she said. She later explained that she was one too.

Now, don't get me wrong; I've met Christians before—but none of them were like him. I rolled my eyes and told her, "Yeah right. I'm sure he's not into all that stuff" (I'm glad I can look back and laugh about this now). As the class continued over the next few weeks, we didn't speak about it again. I just grew anxious every time that particular Thursday night class approached—still unaware of the reason why I had such an odd feeling inside.

Once the quarter came to an end, I decided to send him an email. My feeling never went away, so I figured I would chase it until I found out what it was. I thanked him for the class and shared how I respected his insane level of artistic talent. In addition to being a professor, he worked as an architect and he shared a lot of his personal work with our class. We were all blown away. Nevertheless, we became friends (strictly friends) and entertained the idea of taking our sons to Chuck E. Cheese together one day. His little boy was around Brandon's age at the time, so we figured it would be fun.

Before we could get to that point, however, I needed to know what this "thing" was about him. So I asked. I really couldn't describe what I was trying to ask so it just came out bluntly. "There's something weird about you. I noticed it the first day of class and I've been trying to figure it out ever since."

He responded, "I am a warrior of Jesus Christ." Although these words were simple, they were powerful and hit something deep within the core of my soul. My heart sank in that moment. Not because I was uncomfortable, or even surprised that my fellow classmate was right, but because something deep within in me actually *knew* he was telling the truth.

All the times in my life when I felt an undeniably strong feeling in my heart came flooding back to me. It was as if everything finally made sense out of nowhere, and my understanding was instantly opened. There were several moments during my life in which I heard the gospel prior to this point. Each time, something in me was drawn to it. However, I never cared enough to let it intrigue me. It all led up to this specific moment. I actually *saw* Jesus in someone else. It takes different things for different people, but that's what it took for me. This was the real deal. Question after question after question ran through my mind after his response. What does this mean for me? What does this mean for my son? What does this mean for our lives? I developed a hunger for God. I had to know Him for who He really was, not for the bits and pieces I've heard about Him throughout the years and surely not for what our American culture *wanted* Him to be.

My professor asked me to attend church with him (instead of Chuck E. Cheese) and so I did. When it came time for worship, my face grew hot. It was kind of like when the teacher calls on you in class, and you don't know the answer. Putting my hands up to something I didn't understand felt too awkward. I felt like I belonged, yet didn't belong, at the same time. Perhaps it had something to do with my spirit and flesh fighting one another. It wasn't how things happen on TV, however. There was no running to the altar in tears or screaming "hallelujah!" before dramatically falling onto the floor. I was simply there. Simply there and simply absorbing it all as my heart was being transformed.

I decided to pray after I arrived back home. This time wasn't like when I prayed for Brandon's dad to be alive when I heard he had been shot, or even like any of the other fly-by prayers I may have prayed over the years. This time, I prayed with an open heart and an open mind. My heart understood that I truly did have a Creator, and that I would be forever in debt to Him. He deserved for me to say so much more to Him than I ever had before.

After asking Jesus to enter into my heart, my spirit lit up. It seemed as if it was just sitting in my body all those years before, waiting patiently for me to call it out and seek its purpose. It was relieved that its presence was finally made known. Everything went straight from wondering about God here and there to loving Him with a passion. I prayed vigorously every day from then on, and each time I felt His love flow through my entire being. My late-night bus rides home from class were now spent with my face in the Bible, soaking up as much truth as I could.

Over time, my relationship with Him grew deeper. I began to know Him as if He were right there with me everyday. I could feel His presence all around me in such a way that I couldn't deny His existence even if I wanted to. All of a sudden, He was in the brightness of the stars, in the warmth of the golden sunshine, and even in my son's smile. I began to wonder how I lived so many years without seeing Him. I was truly missing out on so much. He used my professor in order to reveal Himself to me, but that wasn't what opened my heart: it was the simple fact that He actually *loved* me and cared about whether or not I knew Him. The God of the entire universe, who made Heaven and earth, was interested in my crazy, sinning self! Me! Knowing that something so perfect, selfless and powerful, loves *me* unconditionally, still shocks me to my core.

As I began to understand the Bible better and develop more mature prayers, strange things started happening. One time, I had a very strong feeling I was going to meet an older man on the bus who was going to share the Word of God with me. For the next few weeks, I thought every guy on the bus was *the* guy. Eventually, I forgot about it—and then it happened.

An old man sat next to me one evening on my way home from class. He smiled and said, "God sure did make a beautiful world, huh?" I agreed, thinking nothing of it. Then he said, "Take out your Bible." I took it out without hesitation, now remembering what the Lord clearly spoke to me weeks before. The man began to give me advice about very specific things that I was currently facing in my life at the time. He guided me through scriptures while explaining them. It was such a huge moment for me, I wrote everything down. When we arrived at my stop, he simply said, "have a good night and remember what I told you."

These situations not only became normal over time, they became expected. I walked in the spirit daily, actually expecting to hear from God because, well, we were just that tight! He was my Father, my Creator, my Savior and my homie. I'll never forget how excited I was when I first learned that prayer actually *does* work. It was absolutely fascinating to me to be able to make a prayer list and watch each prayer actually be answered. Oh the feeling I felt when I'd be able to grab my pen and check those prayers off. What's even better was that I didn't have to do anything but make my requests known to Him and spend time with Him. He did all the work!

Understanding the way Jesus loved me motivated me to love others to the best of my ability *(Luke 6:31)*. It wasn't easy though, and it still isn't. In fact, it's one of my hardest struggles, loving how *He* loves. However, once I started opening my heart in hopes of becoming more like Him, even more amazing things began happening. He led me to forgive the man who killed my son's father, although I never deemed that possible *(Matthew 19:26)*. One day, I eagerly wrote him a long letter and sent it to him in prison. I told him I forgave him and that the Lord loves him very deeply. Most importantly, I actually *meant* every word and I truly wanted him to forgive himself too, if he carried any guilt. I prayed my letter would show him how powerful Gods grace really is. Now don't get me wrong, I didn't paint a perfect picture of unicorns and sunshine; I was still very honest about my pain as well as the pain of knowing my son will never get to know his father. The letter was full of raw emotion and God's truth. I never heard back from him, so I'm not sure if he received it or not. Years later, I heard he was shot and killed soon after his release from prison. All I can do is hope and pray that his heart was transformed in time, as no sin is too great for God's forgiveness. Nevertheless, God changed my life in such a dramatic way; it often became difficult to even recognize myself at times. I became a totally different person, but I really enjoyed the "new me" (2 Corinthians 5:17).

As I mentioned in the letter, I didn't believe I would ever have any more children. Given my circumstances at the time, I actually had no desire to, understandably so. Now I am happily married and we have *four* children, including Brandon of course. He is currently twelve years old. It's not always a fun age, but he's such an awesome kid. The Lord blessed him with charisma, a great sense of humor, wittiness and so much athletic talent. He's even a pretty good artist like his mom, but he doesn't have an interest in pursuing art (someone please shove a stake into my heart). In addition, he's the best big brother I know. Aside from all the normal wrestling and teasing, he is extremely nurturing and protective of his younger siblings. I really enjoy watching the way he interacts with them and I know he will make a phenomenal father one day.

Marriage was another thing I didn't envision for my future back then. Boy, am I glad I was wrong about that one! My husband is the most amazing man I've ever known. Plus, there is nothing in this world that will teach you more about yourself and give you a greater opportunity to practice selflessness and exemplify Christ than marriage will. If people only knew how deep the sanctity and unity of such a commitment really is, it wouldn't be taken as lightly as it is these days. Marriage was like a beautiful sculpture that the Lord made, but humans took it and melted it down. They re-sculpted it into new shapes and sizes so many times, that there's barely any trace left of its original design. If it's so easy for us to marvel at the beautiful Earth He made, why are we so quick to alter everything else He created? The world seems so eager to remove His fingerprints off of His own property.

We need to remember that life is so much more than what we experience in our own little worlds. Everything we have, including the very air we breathe, is because of *Him*. Therefore, we will forever be in debt to Him. Ironically, His mindset is not focused on that at all. Instead, He pours out unconditional love and forgiveness on us and never looks back *(Psalm 103:12, 1 John 1:9)*. Our relationship with Him should be based on our own free will and desire to love Him, because He first loved us *(1 John 4:19)*. In other words, even if it's hard to put our own desires aside, He's more than worth it. Spending eternity with Him is worth everything, and the sacrifices you may make in order to serve Him in the meantime will not go unrewarded.

Although I've made more bad decisions than I can count, He still believes I am worth loving. He has changed my life in ways I never deemed possible. Is everything perfect? Absolutely not, nor will it ever be. There will always be areas in need of improvement, and I can only pray for Him to search my heart and reveal those flaws to me *(Psalm 139:23)*. I will still make mistakes and there will always be a possibility that I could face another rough season in my life, like when I was fifteen. The point is, I know for a fact He is with me. I am not ashamed of my past, and I am not fearful of my future *(Proverbs*

31:25). I know He will provide everything I need, from a roof over my head to wisdom for day-to-day living. I am so grateful that He enabled me with the ability to cherish even the smallest things in life and simply live for today *(Matthew 6:34)*.

If you currently know a pregnant teenager or a young mother, love her. Shunning her is only going to do more damage to her spirit, which is the last thing she needs. If you know an adolescent who is always acting out, don't write them off and contribute to their bad reputation. You have no idea what they may be facing. Love them. If you know someone who is promiscuous or chose a path you may not understand, there's a reason. Love them. If you know someone who is always bitter and may seem down right evil at times, there's a reason for that too. Love them. The list goes on and loving them doesn't necessarily mean accepting their decisions and behavior.

Everybody has a story and people often act of their out pain before giving themselves a chance to self-evaluate. After all, we are only human. There's always a reason why people make the decisions they make, but love covers a multitude of sins *(1 peter 4:8)*.

Jesus and YOU

God's love and grace are completely free. Yes, we live in a world where nothing is free—there's always a catch, I know. That's because we are humans almost always acting out of our own selfishness. We constantly have a *what's in it for me* mentality, so we naturally expect God to think that way too. Well, I have news for you: He doesn't! Our minds are so simple compared to the complexity and depth of His. We are merely scratching the surface of His entirety. If you hold Him to human standards, you'll never truly know Him to the extent in which He wants you to.

We are all going to die one day, and no matter how much some of us wish we could avoid that inevitable fact, we simply can't. Although we are all well aware of this, it still seems so easy to push it into the back of our minds as if it's insignificant. Why do we treat our eternity with less priority than what we choose to wear for the day? I know we get comfortable with our hectic little lives, but we must remember that this is all just temporary. You could live for ten more days or ten more years, but you won't live forever without Jesus. If you don't know Him and would like to get to know Him, pray this prayer with me:

God, I want to get to know you. I surrender my heart and my life to you. I profess that I'm a sinner and Jesus is my Lord and Savior. Please give me the courage, strength and wisdom it takes to live a life that honors you from this day forward.

Amen

If you just prayed that prayer, congratulations on literally making the most important decision of your life! You've prayed a sweet and simple declaration of change.

I'm sure you're wondering what's next. Well, just keep living your life and every day, make it a point to talk to Him as if He's your best friend. It may sound cliché, but in all actuality He really is quite the best friend to have. Be real with Him, He knows you better than you know yourself anyway *(Psalm 139, Luke 12:7, Jeremiah 1:5)*. Do some research and find a Bible version that feels comfortable for you. I prefer the King James Version, but that's just me. I find so much beauty in the *thee's, thou's* and *ye's*. Pray before you read and before you seek out a church. Pray before everything. Prayer in even the smallest of situations will make a world of a difference.

Take things day by day and keep your heart wide open. When it gets hard (because there *will* be tough times—especially with the direction this world is headed in), don't be discouraged. Just get into the habit of turning to Him, and you'll soon find yourself entering into a new level of spiritual maturity. In the meantime, remember you are still human. You will still make mistakes (again, God knows I've made my fair share of them). You will still fall short of His glory *(Romans 3:23)* and that's okay. The only difference now is what you do with all that garbage in your heart. You can take it out or let it harbor toxic waste in your mind and end up right back where you started *(Proverbs 26:11)*. Don't hold yourself to insanely high standards; it will just set you up for failure. No one will ever be Jesus, but that's the beauty of it all. His power is made perfect in our weakness *(2 Corinthians 12:9)*. That doesn't mean we should give up on trying to *be* like Him, though. I am typing this book right now all because of someone else's desire to be like Him. Getting that glimpse of Jesus spoke to me so much, it changed my entire life.

God can and will use you too, if you let him. Look at me... "little Nikki from New Ken" (yes, "Nikki" is my nickname to some friends and family even though my real name is Natasha. The names don't go together, I know). Anyhow, yes, little Nikki who always managed to create a bad reputation for herself. I've made horrible decisions time after time and had the worst attitude of anyone I knew. I was very easily angered and always full of rage. But that didn't scare God away. He loved me too much to leave me the way I was. He replaced my heart with a new one and is still working on it to this day.

Well dearest friends, this must come to an end. I really hope you enjoyed reading it. May it bring hope to those who have lost all hope and joy to those who are already familiar with God's faithfulness.

If you are facing a tough time in your life, know that it will not last forever and joy really does come in the morning *(Psalm 30:5)*. Remember, above all else in this book, God loves you like crazy. No matter what you've done in your past, what ugly mess you may be in right now, and even despite your future mistakes, He still loves you. The Creator of the entire universe loves you!

Natasha

Area where the shooting took place. Arnold, Pa

Brandon Lockett Sr.

Brandon and I in our first apartment. Age 4

Brandon's first day of kindergarten

Brandon and "Mee maw." Christmas 2013

Brandon and I. 2016

Printed in the United States
By Bookmasters